Indonesia

ISLANDS OF THE IMAGINATION

Text by Michael Vatikiotis

Photographs by Jill Gocher

PERIPLUS EDITIONS
Singapore • Hong Kong • Indonesia

Published by Periplus Editions (HK) Ltd.

www.periplus.com

Text copyright © 2006 Periplus Editions (HK) Ltd.
Photographs copyright © 2006 Jill Gocher

ISBN 978-0-7946-0329-8

Distributed by
North America, Latin America and Europe
Tuttle Publishing
364 Innovation Drive, North Clarendon, VT 05759-9436, U.S.A.
Tel: 1 (802) 773 8930; Fax: 1 (802) 773 6993
info@tuttlepublishing.com; www.tuttlepublishing.com

Asia Pacific
Berkeley Books Pte Ltd
61 Tai Seng Avenue #02-12, Singapore 534167
Tel: (65) 6280 1330; Fax: (65) 6280 6290
inquiries@periplus.com.sg; www.periplus.com

Indonesia
PT Java Books Indonesia
Kawasan Industri Pulogadung, Jl. Rawa Gelam IV No. 9
Jakarta 13930, Indonesia
Tel: 62 (21) 4682 1088; Fax: 62 (21) 461 0206
crm@periplus.co.id; www.periplus.co.id

Printed in Malaysia

15 14 13 12 11   10 9 8 7 6 5 4 3 2   1110TW

Right: A back lane in Ubud is decorated for a temple festival. The tall bamboo poles by the roadside are known as *penjor*, and are symbols of prosperity. **Opposite:** A farmer waters his cattle in a rice field on the island of Lombok. The Indonesian farmer lives in harmony with these beasts of burden. They help trample the hard pan that holds the water in the fields.

Contents

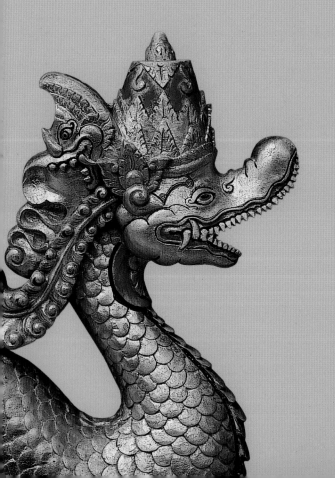

"Men came down the Asian mainland into the archipelago, and crossed to the emerald-green islands around the equator, the Land Under the Rainbow. They came in small dug-outs and outriggers a very long time ago, in the dim and distant past, far beyond the memory of the present Indonesia."

— Mochtar Lubis (1977)

The Land Under the Rainbow

In a world full of color and variety, Indonesia is a galaxy in its own right—thousands of far-flung islands, never ending and always changing, filled with people of all shades and cultures. If the world was ever recreated on a bare canvas, Indonesia would be used as the palette on which to mix the colors.

It's hard to appreciate Indonesia's amazing diversity from the first glimpses of a gray, muddy coastline that marks the approach to Jakarta's international airport. The riot of sound and color begins on the ground. There's the noise, a constant chatter of sing-song Indonesian language with its hard consonants, long rolling "r"s and musically-lilting intonations. There is the ever-present smell of clove-scented *kretek* cigarettes, a hint of fried garlic and onions in the air, and the pungent odor of charcoal. And then there are the smiles. People are always smiling and baring their teeth—great expanses of gum and enamel; there doesn't seem to be any embarrassment when it comes to showing off bad dental work. Welcome to Indonesia.

Indonesia is an archipelagic nation, meaning that it is defined by islands and the seas that separate them. With more than 17,000 islands, it's hard to maintain a mental map of them all. There are of course the larger islands of Java, Sumatra, Sulawesi and Borneo, arrayed like the limbs of a dismembered marionette across the Indian Ocean. Then there are the smaller, farther-flung islands to the east with evocative names like Ternate, Tidore and Banda—islands that once played a larger role in the nation's early history when the world craved cloves and nutmeg to cure and preserve food. Back in the 16th century the seas between these islands were as well known as the waters around Falmouth or Plymouth or Hoorn, from where leaky wooden ships set sail in search of spices. Not much has changed since then in these tiny volcanic specks of greenery, set like emeralds in a sapphire sea.

Being an archipelago helps to sustain Indonesia's variety. There's a natural insularity about the place and people are proud of their distinct traditions and cultures. Languages vary, although one of this country's great achievements has been to disseminate a national language, Bahasa Indonesia, that is understood by all. It's hard to get lost in Indonesia with a few words of Bahasa.

Page 4: The golden dragon, ostensibly a Chinese symbol, is also a symbol of the Sultan of Yogyakarta and his palace or *kraton*.
Page 5: Crowning the summit of the ninth-century Buddhist monument of Borubudur are many aspiring Budddhas or Bodddhisatwas, men on the verge of achieving enlightenment.
Left: A welcoming smile from two boys in an outrigger canoe off the coast near Ujung Pandang in South Sulawesi. Much larger versions of these craft took Indonesia's outer-islanders across oceans as far as Madagascar.
Right: A fisherman patiently plies the waters off Menado, North Sulawesi, in a traditional *perahu*.

Inland Indonesia is cradled by soaring peaks and conical volcanoes, the flatlands between given over almost entirely to rice cultivation. For with more than 235 million people to feed, Indonesia's farmers are pushed to exploit every single square centimeter of land. On the island of Java, the world's most populous island with 125 million people, the landscape is so heavily sculpted by man, that it's hard to find a natural feature.

Here man is master of the environment. Rice cultivation, one of the world's most intensive forms of agriculture, harnesses a confluence of natural forces: the mud that shapes the paddy field and provides organic sustenance; the water than sluices through using gravity as a manager; and the sturdy water buffalo whose feet weigh just enough to preserve the hard pan of mud that holds the water in the paddy field. Then there is the patient farmer, wading the field in a months-long cycle that begins with the planting of green leafy shoots and culminates in the harvest of the yellowed grain stalks. Bent over double, mostly under a scorching sun, there are few occupations anywhere that involve so much manual toil and yet are so critical to man's survival.

Nature, like everything else in Indonesia is colorful and complex. Indonesia's wildlife can be divided into two distinct regions. The British naturalist Alfred Russel Wallace first postulated that there was an imaginary dividing line between

Right: The planting of tender green rice shoots in a previously plowed and flooded field is painstaking work.

Asiatic and Australian fauna. Named after him, the Wallace Line passes between Bali and Lombok islands at its southern end and runs northward from here between Kalimantan and Sula-wesi. It then curves to the east along the southern edge of the Philippines.

Along this line Wallace observed a major break in fauna based on his observations of birds, especially of parrots, throughout the islands in the area. Wallace was puzzled by the fact that Asian birds thrived on the island of Bali, while just 25 kilometers (15 miles) across a narrow strait, the island of Lombok was missing some prominent Asian species. The birds on Lombok were more clearly related to those of New Guinea and Australia than those of Bali. He marked the channel between Bali and Lombok as the divide between two great zoogeographic regions, the Oriental and the Australian. The line also acts as a barrier to Asian species of freshwater fish and large mammals, which cannot be found east of the Wallace Line. It is certainly striking to be traveling in the far-flung eastern province of Papua and come across kangaroos and gum trees.

However, there are many species indigenous to Indonesia, like the "orangutan" (which literally means "man of the jungle" in Indonesian) apes of Sumatra and Kalimantan and the giant "dragon" lizards, which are the only giant reptiles of their kind in the world today roaming free on the island of Komodo. This throwback to the dinosaur age is protected within a heavily guarded national park. Similarly, the one-horned rhinoceros of Java, the wild "banteng" oxen, tigers and many other species are now protected in wildlife reserves.

Indonesia is also home to some of the largest stands of primary tropical rainforest in Asia, and therefore is an important repository of the region's biodiversity. Indonesia's natural beauty makes it a feast for the eyes, and yet what is truly remarkable is how closely man and nature interact in a landscape constantly moulded by man. Perhaps the best-known man-made features are the intricate rice terraces of Java and Bali. Built along the contours of this volcanic landscape, they offer the most efficient way to exploit the land and yet somehow lend more beauty to the scenery. Close up the visitor can wander along the grassy mud-built bunds that rim the terraces and feast one's eyes upon the fluorescent colors of the ripening rice, whilst listening to the relaxing sound of gurgling water as it drains from one terrace to the next. There are few man-made or natural landscapes as pleasing or as friendly to the senses.

The Indonesian archipelago has collected people like a giant colander, as waves of itinerant mariners, passing traders and refugees, invaders and migrants have over the ages passed through or across the seas between these islands. The earliest Indonesians were some of man's earliest forbears. Fossils of

Opposite top: A fierce looking Komodo dragon. Their jaws are alive with bacteria that infect the slightest wound inflicted by the lizard's sharp teeth—and they will attack humans if they smell them nearby.
Opposite bottom: The vast jungles of South Kalimantan. Indonesia's tropical forests, though fast disappearing, are a valuable biological resource.
Right top: The elephant "school" in Lampung, South Sumatra, where elephants are trained to extract timber.
Right bottom: An orangutan observes life from a tree in Gunung Lawang, South Sumatra; these gentle primates are now protected by law.

Opposite: The contrast of light and dark that haunts many Balinese paintings is seen here in stark reality near Ubud.

Above: A farmer stops to rest on the edge of his rice field in Ubud, Bali. Rice cultivation is a labor-intensive task and there is seldom time for idleness.

Right: Rice terraces in Payangan above Ubud, Bali.

Facing page: Classical dancers from the ancient palace or *kraton* in Yogyakarta. Children are taught classical dance from an early age in Central Java—a part of their heritage that reaches back into the pre-Islamic Hindu past.
Above: A Sumatran beauty dressed in wedding finery. West Sumatran women own all landed property in one of the world's only surviving matrilineal societies.

Above: A Buginese girl from South Sulawesi wearing her traditional costume. These proud sea-faring people produce delicate works of filigree and bold textile designs. Their looks are deceiving; fine featured but tough and aggressive. As migrants all over Indonesia they make formidable commercial competitors.

Above: A Balinese temple dancer made up for a performance. Hindu religious ritual and devotion is the source of this island's expressive culture of dance, which is very much alive on Bali today.

"Java Man" (*Pithecanthropus Erectus*) dating back some 500,000 years, were first discovered in Central Java, suggesting that some of man's earliest ancestors inhabited the island of Java. The "original" human inhabitants of these islands were black-skinned relatives of the Australian aborigines and present-day Papuans. Later migrations to the Indonesian archipelago have been traced as far back as 3,000–500 B.C. They were lighter-skinned peoples from what is now southern China who arrived by boat via Taiwan and the Philippines and have been credited with introducing to the region new Stone, Bronze and Iron Age cultures as well as the Austronesian languages and rice agriculture. Recent discoveries on the island of Flores have uncovered evidence of an early humanoid species (*Homo flore-siensis*) that stood no taller than 90 cetimeters (three feet) high.

Later on, Indonesia came under the influence of the Indian civilization through the gradual influx of Indian traders in the first century A.D. Their arrival saw great Hindu and Buddhist empires emerge. By the seventh century, a powerful Buddhist kingdom called Sriwijaya located on the southeastern coast of south-central Sumatra managed to expand its influence throughout much of Southeast Asia. The thirteenth century saw the rise of the Majapahit Empire in East Java, which united the whole of what is now modern-day Indonesia and parts of the Malay peninsula, and ruled for two centuries.

Later still, Muslim Indian traders and merchants laid the foundations for the gradual spread of Islam to the region, starting from Aceh at the northern tip of Sumatra and then moving to Malacca and the north coast of Java much later. Islam spread slowly and did not replace Hinduism and Buddhism as the dominant religion until the end of the 16th century. Small Muslim kingdoms did indeed develop, but none could resist the strength and persistence of the Europeans that followed.

The Portuguese came first, rough traders wearing wool and bearing the cross. In 1511, Portuguese trading posts were established in the strategic commercial center of Malacca on the Malay peninsula and it was from here that they began to reach out and establish trading posts along the north coast of Java and of course in the eastern Spice Islands. The Dutch followed at the turn of the 16th century and succeeded in ousting the Portuguese. The Dutch expanded their control of the entire archipelago in the 17th and 18th centuries and retained it for the most part until the outbreak of World War II in 1942.

As a result of this complex history, almost 600 different languages and dialects flourish in Indonesia today. Although the majority of the population are Muslims, some 85%, there are also thriving communities of Christians, Buddhists and Hindus—as well as animists. Overlaying the main religious groups are innumerable local beliefs and traditions associated with place and history. This all makes for a kalaedoscopic array of rituals and customs, each associated with its own colorful costume and design, ranging from the elaborate courtly dress of the Javanese to the golden horned headgear of the Minangkabau in West Sumatra.

Opposite: A Kenyah Dayak warrior chief in the lower Mahakam River in East Kalimantan. In ancient times victorious warriors lopped off the heads of their foes and ate their hearts and livers fresh.
Top right: A welcoming dance at Tanjung Isuy, East Kalimantan.
Bottom right: Longhouse entrance with ornate carvings at Tanjung Isuy, East Kalimantan.

Left: Serene and awe-inspiring Mount Bromo in East Java. This desolate and deserted moon-like landscape looks oddly out of place on the world's most populous island.
Top: A lonely horse rider on Mount Bromo's "Sea of Sand."
Above: A "sulphur-picker" at work in the Papandayan volcano in West Java.

Clockwise from top left: Young couple in traditional dress from Bengkulu, South Sumatra; *Legong* dancers from Bali, the dance that conjures up the vision of angels; A Minangkabau girl from Padang who will eventually inherit all her family's property in one of the world's only truly matrilineal societies; Warriors from Nias off the coast of Sumatra, where stone leaping is a traditional sport.

Clockwise from top left: Horse dancers in East Java; Traditional water containers in East Nusa Tenggara; The Tari Topeng, or mask dance in Cirebon on the north coast of Java. Many of these dances originated in the courtly culture of Java and were performed for local kings; Nias maidens dancing.

Different Islands, Different Cultures

"The revolution that gave birth to the Indonesian people and the nation that is Indonesia erased the centuries-long slate of colonialism and restored self-respect and honor to millions of this world's inhabitants. It changed the map of power and affected, to some degree, the thinking of people around the world. It changed the world itself."

— Pramoedya Ananta Toer

There is something alluring about a people who look you straight in the eye. Walk down just about any street in Indonesia and their eyes will meet yours, almost never averted. It's not so much a stare as an engagement, for Indonesians are a naturally gregarious people. Whether it's the young store clerk, the elderly food vendor, or the lady selling chilies in the market, every encounter, however fleeting, is full of warmth—and often more. Take the railway porter outside Bandung station who argues volubly with a complete stranger that the trains will never run on time. "It's about politics and money," he says enigmatically. Or there's the taxi driver in Jakarta who honestly believes that dreams determine our lives. "When I dream, I know what lies ahead."

A simple event can be filled with mystery and knowledge. Indonesians possess an endearing natural curiosity; perhaps it stems from the huge variety of peoples and cultures that comprise the national mosaic.

A market place is where the movement of people and goods intersects. Here among baskets of aromatic fruits, pungent spices, and fresh vegetables, women reign supreme. The covered markets are filled with the sound of their cackles and catcalls; bargaining is fierce and noisome. Sitting all day on a low bench or woven bamboo mat surrounded by baskets of produce and clouds of flies, the Indonesian woman bears the burden of commerce and is the fulcrum of everyday existence.

Women generally have an important status in Indonesian society. In some localities ancient matrilineal practices still prevail, as in West Sumatra where men have limited property and inheritance rights and all the family clans are led by women. But more generally it is women who manage family affairs, conduct commerce, and act as the anchor for family and society. The Javanese, for example, believe that husband and wife should work together as a team. Despite the male bias in the majority Islamic religion, wealth is equally shared and inherited and children for the most part show more respect and affection towards their mothers. There is a spirit of independence about Indonesian women, who generally make all the important decisions in any household. Men are perceived as useless, inclined if allowed, to spend all their time gossiping, smoking clove cigarettes and squandering whatever money they are given on card games or

Page 22: A Muslim in Malang, East Java, wears the white cap signifying that he has made the important pilgrimage to Mecca.
Page 23: A Tari Topeng, or mask dance troupe in Cirebon on the north coast of Java.
Left: Women dominate the markets in Java, as seen here in the fresh vegetable market in central Java. Their laughter pierces the heat and they are always ready to engage in conversation to lure the buyer to their wares.

cock-fighting. Walk through any urban or rural neighborhood and it is the men you see lounging in the shade; the women are almost always hard at work indoors or tending to children.

At the same time, women face the most obstacles in Indonesian society—they are twice as likely to be illiterate as men, find it harder to get jobs in the formal labor force, and suffer higher rates of unemployment. Women have more limited opportunities than men. The younger they marry, the more successful they are in giving birth to children, the more likely they are to find security in a family unit. Divorce rates and the attrition rates of marriages are very high—averaging around 50% of all marriages. In part this is brought about by economic necessity. Many young men in rural areas marry at harvest time, fall into debt, and then divorce a few months later during the slack season. Migration and forced separation also contribute to broken homes.

Then there is the creative side. Women are the weavers, designers and creators of some of the most exquisite Indonesian handicrafts. They pore over the hot wax that helps create elaborately designed batik cloth; they embroider and weave, stitch and sew and then what emerges creates the allure and enhances the beauty of women who are already endowed so well by nature.

Everyday life in Indonesia is marked by the passage of rituals. There are the needs of religion—days of atonement, fasting, celebration and the passage of life. Then there are rituals of place and local spirits to appease. Finally, in some areas, there are the

Right: The pungent smell of garlic, shallots and chilies are ever-present in this Cirebon marketplace. The fresh market is a fixture of all Indonesian towns and cities. They offer the lowest prices and are unthreatened by the spread of supermarket chains.

Clockwise from top left: Cockfighters preen their prize birds in Ubud, Bali. The sport remains popular in rural areas, where a man's fighting cock is often his most valued possession; Balinese temple dancers begin learning at a young age; Young girls at a dance practice in Ubud, Bali; Gamelan players in a Bali temple. The crashing chords are the main accompaniment to Balinese dance.

vestigial rituals of royalty and nobility, for Indonesia is one of the few republics in the world to tolerate a thriving courtly culture.

In a lush tropical climate, very few of these rituals are conducted indoors, and given the country's natural abundance, much of the paraphernalia of ritual is drawn from the natural environment. The banana tree trunk becomes a solid base in which the shadow puppeteer plants his characters; the coconut frond serves as the latticework of elaborate offerings for the Hindu Balinese; and rice is sacred to almost all.

The great source of inspiration for much of Indonesian culture and ritual lies in the great Hindu epics, the Ramayana and the Mahabharata. An epic of Homeric proportions, the Mahabharata tells of kings and nobles in a great struggle for the cosmos, while the Ramayana is a more straightforward epic poem that tells the story of King Rama, his wife Sita and brother Laksamana. Both stories came to Indonesia with Indian traders who also brought early Hinduism to Indonesia. Their characters and themes remain deeply embedded in Javanese and Balinese culture, where these epic tales form the basis for the popular *wayang kulit*, or shadow puppet theatre. But the role of these epics goes beyond that of storytelling, and has come to embody a set of values and cultural aestheticism drawing on the ancient caste system of India, with

Top right: Temple dancers in Bali bearing incense and offerings. Bali's Hinduism is unique and still commands widespread dedication and devotion on the island, despite the influx of foreign tourists and commercial values. The Balinese have managed to harness their culture and religion to the tourist industry and keep the essence of Balinese identity very much alive.
Bottom right: Village women in Bali carry their offerings to the Hindu temple, or puri. Everything associated with temple rites is made from natural ingredients.

Court retainers in Yogyakarta serve the sultan for virtually no pay. In return they receive food, shelter and clothing and a lifetime of security at the heart of the old Javanese culture. It may seem as if they sit around most of the day smoking pungent clove cigarettes, but they are guardians of an elaborate court culture that stretches back six hundred years.

These retainers in the Yogyakarta palace hold up elaborately-carved leather characters from the shadow puppet theatre, or *wayang kulit*. Performances of the shadow puppet theater can last all night long, and feature tales drawn from the Ramayana and Mahabharata Hindu epics.

its warrior knights, and high priests. These divisions and the symbiosis between them infuses Indonesian culture and morality. There is something powerful and emblematic about the decision by Rama to cast off his noble robes and assume the life of a humble hermit in the forest. "The people of Ayodhya wept as Rama, Sita and Laksamana passed from the city," runs one oral version of the epic poem. "As the chariot went from sight, Dasaratha (Rama's father) cried, 'Rama! Rama! Do not leave me.' In time, Dasaratha lost the will to live. His heart simply gave out. Ayodhya mourned the loss of their king."

The majority Javanese, more than 90 million of the country's 235 million people, divide their culture into several distinct regional variations. There is the distinct north coast culture that extends from Cirebon just west of Jakarta all the way east to Gresik in East Java. The east Javanese are considered rough and less refined that their cousins in the courtly centers of Yogyakarta and Solo. Common to all of these variations is a complex language characterized by different levels of refinement determined by social status. There are more than a dozen ways to say the word "spouse," for example.

In character, the Javanese are reserved and usually withhold their real emotions, placing great emphasis on inner strength and

Left: Offerings prepared for the Sekaten festival at the palace in Yogyakarta. Sekaten commemorates the birth of the Prophet Muhammad. It is marked by a procession of sacred gamelan orchestras. Locals believe that by celebrating Sekaten and in particular listening to gamelan, they will be rewarded with good health and prosperity.
Opposite: Palace guards in a colorful procession to mark the annual Sekaten festival in the palace of Yogyakarta.

Clockwise from top left: Pig roasting feast in the Baliem valley of West Papua. For Papuans the pig is a major source of protein, along with tree grubs and fish; Toraja lady dressed for a festival in South Sulawesi; Market girls in Lombok; Diamond miner, central Kalimantan.

self-control. Children show great respect to their parents, and people of aristocratic lineage are deferred to with a most obsequious display of groveling. Such gentility is compensated by a mischievous sense of humor, often at their own expense, especially at humble levels of society.

The Javanese are generous and engaging. In art and culture they stand head and shoulders above their outer islander cousins, although the feeling of superiority has been a hindrance to national integration. Indonesia's founding father Sukarno recognized the dangers and made a dialect of the Malay language spoken on Sumatra the national language, instead of Javanese.

Outside the realm of mainstream Malay and Javanese culture there is a dizzying array of tribal and localized traditions. From the Indic and Arab traditions of Islam, to the cargo cults of Melanesia, Indonesia is host to all the spiritual and cultural influences that swirl through Asia. The astonishing thing is that so many of these traditions survive after 60 years of unitary nationhood. Whilst there is an overarch-ing Indonesian identity and language, that's often little in evidence when you visit islands like Sumbawa, or the far flung extremities of the republic like Ambon or Aceh.

Indeed, the Acehnese have been struggling for independence for decades, whilst in Papua, there have been demands for a plebiscite on self-rule. Such is the strength of local tradition and identity that more recently Indonesia has enacted a comprehensive set of laws to ensure a less centralized system of government and more autonomy for the regions. For many places like the old sultanate of Kutai in East Kalimantan, that means a chance to revive old traditions of self-rule, which in the Indonesian context hasn't always meant independence, but merely acknowledgement of a central government, so long as local traditions and culture are respected. For Indonesia's almost 400 ethnic groups and distinct peoples, a sense of dignity is all that is required and for the most part they would all prefer to live under the rainbow that is modern Indonesia.

Above: A broad-nosed Dani tribesman with classic Melanesian features in West Papua, the easternmost island of Indonesia. The Dani people of the Baliem valley were the last substantial civilization to be discovered on earth. It was only in the 1940s that the 140,000-strong group of tribes in the highlands of New Guinea were found by the outside world.

Clockwise from top left: Village elder from the island of Nias off west Sumatra; Boys dressed for the temple in Bali; Batak Ladies in North Sumatra; Tanjung Isuy villager in East Kalimantan.

Clockwise from top left: A young Kei islander shelters from the rain; A coconut seller works the beach on the southern coast of Lombok; A woman trader rows her boat in the water market in Banjarmasin, South Kalimantan; A Buginese boy in South Sulawesi.

"To me, as to so many who have beheld Java not with the
bodily eye alone, it must still remain a land of dreams and
fancies, the enchanted isle where innocent beliefs and
gladsome thoughts, such as are the privilege of children
and childlike nations, still have their happy home."

— Augusta de Wit (1912)

Java: The Enchanted Isle

The flickering flame of a small oil lamp is all that illuminates the taut screen against which the magical tale of life unfolds. From behind the screen a man's voice imitates the whining of a fearful retainer. Suddenly, with a loud tap, his tone drops, the voice transformed into the booming baritone of a fierce knight warrior. A dark shadow appears on the edge of the screen. "Heh, heh, heh," the man laughs. Set against the screen, the delicate leather latticework of the puppet retainers quiver and tremble echoing the fear in the hearts of the characters they represent.

Night after night, for more than a thousand years, countless generations have sat enthralled by one of the greatest tales the world has ever known, the Mahabharata. The *wayang kulit* or shadow puppet theater is probably one of the oldest continuous traditions of storytelling in the world. It is also offers a window on the cultural core of Indonesia, the island of Java.

Java lies like a long hyphen along the southern edge of Southeast Asia, connecting the two worlds of India and China and underlining a region of immense and fascinating variety. The ancient Greeks believed that a place the Indians referred to as Yavadvipa ("The Island of Grain") possessed a climate too inhospitable for human habitation; they could not have been more wrong. From the dawn of history, this land of volcanoes and rich black lava soil, was a fertile seedbed for a variety of peoples and their cultures. Today with more than 125 million people, Java is the most populous island in the world, host to more than half a dozen cities of more than a million people, that serves as the cultural hearth of Indonesia.

The gateway to this magical land for foreigners has always been the old 14th century port of Sunda Kelapa, which the Dutch renamed Batavia when they arrived in the early 1600s, and upon which the modern Indonesian capital of Jakarta now stands. The city's extensive coastal anchorage is sheltered by an array of tropical islets—several hundred of them. Today's modern city of over 12 million people is a forest of modern office towers set amidst a sprawl of traditional red-tiled, single-storey urban village structures. Its modern highways fan out of the city and lead the traveler into the heart of one of the world's most fascinating cultures.

Page 36: Nightly performances of the traditional Javanese *wayang wong* theater still take place in Central Java.
Page 37: Brightly-dressed palace guards in Yogyakarta, the ancient Javanese capital near Borobudur.
Left: The Freedom monument in central Jakarta was erected by the country's first president, Sukarno, and is capped with gold. The monument sits in the center of an old Dutch colonial park that has since become a central meeting place for Jakartans on weekends.

Clockwise from top left: Planet Hollywood is one of Jakarta's many popular nightspots; Jakarta's "Golden Triangle" is lined with glass towers housing banks and corporations. Most were completed before the 1997 financial crisis; By night this city of nearly 12 million pulsates with traffic and almost never sleeps; The city's main circle on Jalan Thamrin in front of the famous Hotel Indonesia, is a central focus for popular protests.

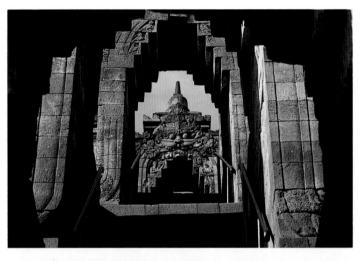

Left: A Buddha image overlooks the glory of Borobudur, one of the greatest Buddhist temples ever built. Thought to have been completed in the ninth century A.D., it consists of many layers of intricately-carved lava rock culminating in a single stupa in the shape of a lotus flower.
Top: View of the stairs leading up to the top of Borobudur.
Above: Detail from a carving of the Buddha teaching along one of the many galleries lining the sides of Borobudur.

The gamelan orchestra looks like a collection of kitchen pots and pans, but the sound it can produce has the power to entrance the listener. With its distinctive five or seven tone tuning system, the music is endlessly variable and concerts can last for hours. The players seemingly have no connection with one another, but in fact they follow a strict set of rules and direction. You know when the orchestra is playing well when you have fallen into a semi trance-like state and the graceful movements of the dancers seem like they are part of a dream.

Java has acquired its intricate culture through a long process of eclectic accretion. In the earliest years of its history, Java acted as a waystation for Chinese pilgrims traveling to the holy Hindu and Buddhist sites of India, or for monks on their sojourn to China. In the 5th century A.D., a Chinese pilgrim Fa-hsien observed that there was nothing pure or notable about the Buddhism he saw practiced in Java. Yet, by the 8th century, Javanese kings and princes could boast of political influence as far afield as Cambodia, and in the 12th century, the Javanese kingdom of Majapahit was one of the only local Southeast Asian principalities to repulse a Chinese invasion.

Modern Java was shaped by the interplay between long-established Hindu-Buddhist civilizations, the arrival of Islam, and the rude interruption of the Dutch—who arrived in Java

Left: Players in the royal gamelan strike their large gongs in Yogyakarta. The cloth headscarf, or *blankon*, is made of batik and starched into shape.
Opposite: A performance of the Ramayana accompanied by the royal gamelan in Yogyakarta. These performances are punctuated by dramatic music and acrobatic dance movements.

in the early 1600s and colonized the island for over 300 years. You can see this most clearly in the batik cloth that is the hallmark of Java's rich heritage of textile design. Carefully traced on cotton with the help of melted beeswax, the figurative motifs of Chinese and Indian sacred tradition dance against the colors and geometric designs inspired by modern Islam and the floral motifs favored by Europeans.

The social reality is just as enmeshed, although tensions lie just beneath the surface. It took several hundred years for Islam, which came to Java's north coast on the coattails of the Muslim Indian textile trade, to penetrate and overcome the intricate Hindu-Buddhist court rituals of Central Java. Even today, a strong syncretism is evident in the courtly dances and the characters of the *wayang*. Javanese culture is suffused with superstition that harks back to the spirits of ancient times. In modern Central Java, the current ruling Sultan would never dream of making a decision without first consulting the Goddess of the Southern Seas.

Java's royal culture, its surviving sultans and their courts, offer another stark reminder of the island's curious cultural ambiguity. Java was the heart of the Republican revolution that overthrew Dutch colonial rule, yet for a while the royal capital of Yogyakarta, with its feudal monarchy, served as the

Top left: Dancers in Cirebon on the north coast of Java perform the Tari Topeng, or mask dance.
Bottom left: Young girls in the Arab quarter of Surabaya. Arabs have settled in Indonesia since at least the ninth century.
Opposite: Painted fishing boats in Cirebon harbor, among the most ancient ports in all of Java.

republican capital—and the Sultan as its staunchest supporter. This shrewd move on the part of the royals, helps explain the paradox of a thriving monarchy in the heart of a Republic. Today's sultans, in Yogyakarta, Solo, and Cirebon keep a low political profile—though the Sultan of Yogyakarta is also head of the city's administration and was briefly considered a presidential candidate. Their survival acts as a reference point for the Javanese, who remain wedded to the ancient rituals and artefacts of a bygone era when kings and kingdoms took grand titles like "central spike of the universe." As for Islam, the survival of pre-Islamic culture helps moderate religious fervor in a culture where rose petals are strewn on graves and in the holiest of religious communities along the north coast of Java, where Muslims don't eat beef—just like Hindus.

Opposite: The Jamik Mosque in Sumenep on the island of Madura, off the coast of East Java, one of the small corners of Indonesia's surviving royal cultures.
Top right: Palace guards from Madura.
Bottom right: The Kerapan Sapi, Madura's famous annual bull run.
Pages 48–49: A panoramic view of the Parahyangan ("Abode of the Gods") mountains, in West Java, near Bandung.

Bali: The Paradise Isle

"Life is an offering. Life is art. May all this remain eternal."
— Arthanegara (1982)

In the Indonesian galaxy of cultures, Bali is one of the brightest stars. This tear-shaped island with its undulating rice terraces and bamboo groves, placid inland lakes and surf-pounded beaches sits in a shimmering azure sea overlooked by the silent bulk of an ancient volcano. It's almost as if nature has produced its own microchip crammed full of environmental splendor. Paradise is the word that most easily springs to mind—a paradise that never seems to get lost in the headlong rush towards development. This is the central paradox of Bali. How can a culture so steeped in a mystical past manage to survive the ravages of a modern consumer society?

The answer lies in the ability of its people to blend and synthesize the old with the new, so that an exquisite Balinese dance or stone carving becomes a tourist attraction and earns income, and these skills and traditions are harnessed to the livelihood of the Balinese and do not atrophy.

The natural splendor of Bali is best appreciated inland from the coast, away from the noise and traffic of the tourist hubs to the south, away from the bustle of tourist touts and the incessant cries of "transport." Take the road north from the capital Denpasar to the foothills of Bali's mountainous spine, and a town called Bedugul on the shores of a tranquil mountain lake. On the lake's northeastern shore sits a temple dedicated to the lake goddess who is worshipped as a source of fertility.

Nothing is more tranquil and relaxing than simply soaking up the scenery of Bali, and yet this island of more than 3 million people is no bigger than 5,600 square kilometers (2,162 square miles). This works because the Balinese have managed to harness nature so perfectly to their way of life. There are huge banyan trees in villages and temple grounds, tamarind and flame trees sheltering the roads, and more than a dozen species of coconut palms and varieties of bamboo that provide the basic building blocks of decorative landscaping.

And then there are the flowers. The fragrances of hibiscus, bougainvillea and jasmine fills the air. Magnolia, frangipani and orchids add a profusion of color to the simplest of gardens, along roads and in temple grounds. Flowers are also used as decorations in temples, on statues, as offerings for the gods, and during prayers. Even the dullest of statues, when graced with a bright red hibiscus flower, seems to come to life.

Page 51: Balinese children become active participants in village rituals from a very early age—learning to make and present offerings, play music and dance at frequent village temple festivals
Left: The serenity of a lakeside Hindu temple on the shore of Lake Bratan in Bedugul, central Bali. There are few places in the world that combine man-made and natural grace so effortlessly.

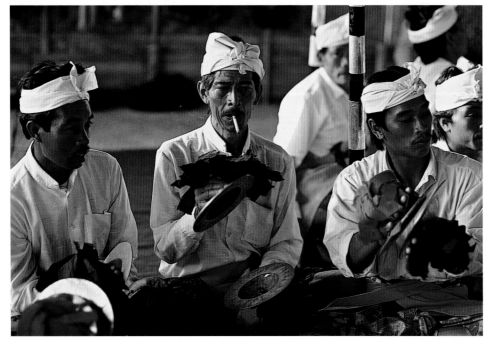

The majority of Balinese are Hindu, a throwback to the early Indian religious influence that swept over these islands. The Balinese Hindu calendar is jammed full of festivals and holy days, and to be a practicing Hindu in Bali is a constant round of obligations towards the local village *puri* or temple. To the tourists, these fleeting glimpses of ritual life in Bali seem quaint, but to the Balinese they help bring order to life and reinforce family and community bonds.

The temple festival is a riot of sound and color. Music is provided by the Balinese gamelan. Punctuated by crashing cymbals and the rapid staccato of coordinated drum and gong beats, the gamelan in Bali is a spectacular percussive experience. The explosive chords and long sustained hammering of gongs serve to proclaim life and act as a counterpoint to the tranquility of the surroundings. Then the dancers emerge, their movements as precise as clockwork, their make-up and costumes transporting the audience to a world of mythical gods and spirits. The great Baris Gede dance will be performed by men in most temple festivals. It's a stylized display of martial prowess involving spears and lances and is often performed these days to welcome guests.

Away from the climatic sights and sounds of ritual devotion, Bali offers one of the most tranquil living environments.

Top left: The majestic Baris Gede dance performed in Kintamani. The orchestra keeps up a fierce tempo to match the stylized aggression of the warrior.
Bottom left: Gamelan players bang out their percussive rhythms.
Opposite: A gamelan orchestra rehearses on the footsteps of a magnificent temple in Ubud.

Left: Women carrying offerings arrive at a temple festival in the village of Batuan.

Above: A back lane in Ubud is decorated for a temple festival. The tall bamboo poles by the roadside are known as *penjor*, and are symbols of prosperity.

Opposite: Inside a temple at Badung, young Balinese maidens make their devotions during a festival day. On these days, it is not unusual for Balinese to make visits to the temple more than once a day.

Harnessing their acute sense of beauty and artisanal skills, the Balinese have crafted some of the most beautiful places of human habitation anywhere in the world. Where else can you lie under a thatched roof staring at an exquisitely carved stone wall and then let the eye wander over hibiscus and frangipani blooms before focusing on undulating rice terraces in middle distance. Even the most modest of bungalows in the artisans' town of Ubud offers stunning views of the Campuan River valley, its deep gorge lined with delicately carved rice terraces and cluttered with luxuriant bamboo groves. The scenery is so inviting and luscious, it almost seems wasteful to sleep. Bali style is now so influential that hotel resorts around the world borrow some element of this most natural of architectural styles. It could be the hibiscus flower placed on stone statues, or the palm fronds used to decorate even the simplest items like key rings or tip trays. Bali invites the world to relax and observe the wisdom of its culture.

Top left: The relaxing interior of the Bagus Jati health spa located along the road to Kintamani above Ubud.
Left: A private bungalow set amidst a landscaped garden at the Four Seasons Hotel, Sayan west of Ubud.
Right: The beachfront bar at the Four Seasons Hotel in Jimbaran, facing Bali's international airport.

Above: A man-made mosaic of rice fields orders the volcanic Bali landscape.
Left: Rice terraces seen against the serene volcanic backdrop of Mount Agung in East Bali. The undulating forms present one of the most impressive man-made features in the world, and they play a vital role in helping to distribute water to ensure an abundant crop.
Pages 62–63: Young boys enjoy an evening stroll along Bali's fabled Kuta beach.

Indonesia's Outer Islands: To The Ends Of The Earth

"He looked at the brown and sparkling solitude of the flowing water, of the water flowing ceaseless and free in a soft, cool murmur of ripples at his feet. The world seemed to end there."
— Joseph Conrad (1896)

The rickety sailboats that line the quayside at Jakarta's Sunda Kelapa harbor look more like museum pieces than anything else. Yet these vessels with their graceful lines, and not so graceful crews, are the mainstay of the inter-island shipping that keeps people and goods moving between the archipelago's 17,000 islands. If you want to island-hop eastward from Java to Bali, to Lombok, and then on to Sulawesi and the Maluku Islands, or farther northwestwards to Sumatra, then hop aboard a *phinisi* with its tattered sails and rough-hewn, chain-smoking crew. Sailing the seas between these islands is perhaps the last way to experience life much as it would have been for Indonesians before the modern age. The stars guided mariners and they were at the mercy of the wind; the threat from marauding pirates was ever-present. Hop aboard and take a tour of Indonesia's outer islands. The diversity is almost endless and the magic beckons.

North Sumatra lies at the westernmost tip of Indonesia, the first landfall for traders arriving from India and the Middle East centuries ago. This is the land of the Bataks, one of the largest indigenous groups in Indonesia, comprising six major groups with a total population of 3 million.

They are a colorful and brash people, known to speak their mind. They take strange names like Kennedy and Roosevelt, often naming their children after events.

Batak architecture is unique and enduring. The traditional communal houses have three levels, which correspond to the three levels of their universe: the upper world, the middle world, and the lower world. The high roof represents the upper world, the realm of the gods. The living level symbolizes the middle world where humans dwell. The space for animals below the living level represents the lower world, believed to be the home of a mythological dragon.

The Batak people live around Lake Toba, a 100-kilometer (62-mile)-long stretch of water that is actually the caldera of a collapsed volcano, the result of one of the most massive volcanic explosions ever to take place some 80,000 years ago. Today the lake is a major tourist attraction.

Page 64: A solid gold ceremonial mask from the islands of southwestern Maluku province in eastern Indonesia.
Page 65: Wooden sailing craft like these continue to carry valuable cargoes to the outer islands of Indonesia.
Top left: Batak culture is asserted strongly in the architecture of traditional dwellings such as this one on Simanindo in the middle of Lake Toba.
Left: Although a strongly patriarchal society, Batak women play a leading role in commerce and are canny merchants.
Right: The placid shores of Lake Toba belie its fiery volcanic origins. This lake was formed 80,000 years ago by the largest volcanic explosion ever.

A thousand kilometers to the east, in Torajaland, it is the way of death, rather than the way of life, which makes this inland enclave of South Sulawesi so interesting and colorful. Situated 300 kilometers (186 miles) north of the port capital of Makasar, the mainly Christian Toraja community believes that the dead don't simply depart; they hang around, literally.

Death in Torajaland is more like a life ritual. For the dead are considered part of the living world, their souls watching over the living. They are given elaborate funerals and often not properly sent on their way until enough money has been found for an elaborate feast. The souls of the dead in Torajaland ascend to heaven on the backs of slaughtered pigs and buffaloes—so a proper funeral can be an expensive affair.

Like so many of Indonesia's component cultures, Torajans enjoy a degree of dissimilarity and uniqueness that suggests a long period of neglect. Yet today the area is a frequently visited tourist spot. Modern influence may prevail in the shape of consumerism and communication, but in fact the role of tourism as a cultural preservative cannot be underestimated. The fact that people trek all the way to see Torajans and their unique culture helps reinforce those traditions the tourists want to see. Call it ersatz, but at least it remains much the same as it always was.

Opposite: A funeral procession in Torajaland is only the start of a long ritual to remember the dead.
Top right: Preparing for the funeral feast, a costly occasion that Torajans save a lifetime for.
Bottom right: Although mainly Christian, Torajan society retains a strong bond with its animist past.

The immense island of Borneo is the world's third largest, and nature is firmly in command here. Unlike Java, which is the world's most populous island, here on Borneo vast tracts of primary rain forest drained by a dense network of rivers, reduce the human population to mere specks on the surface.

Borneo evokes the sheer power of nature; it is a storehouse of energy in the form of oxygen released into the atmosphere. It is a warehouse of biodiversity and is increasingly regarded as one of the world's greatest repositories of the genetic variation that keeps our world free of incurable disease.

Along the mighty Mahakam River in Indonesian East Kalimantan, over 1,000 kilometers (600 miles) long and a kilometer (half a mile) wide in places, nature dwarfs the riverboats that ply these waters. People cling to shelters along its banks and never quite seem in control of their destiny. Tall dipterocarps tower above like stern sentinels, while at nightfall the darkness is total. This is Joseph Conrad's other heart of darkness. The great Mahakam was the setting for some of the most hypnotic of his stories, like *Almayer's Folly*, *Lord Jim* and *Outcast of the Islands*. Conrad deployed the fast moving river and the dramatic backdrop of the jungle to explore man's inhumanity and weakness. Perhaps it was the Borneo landscape that led him in this direction. This is certainly no place for dreams of Promethean idealism.

Left: Banjarmasin is a bustling town in Borneo which hovers over the waters of the Barito river.
Opposite: Early morning on the great Mahakam River in East Kalimantan. This wide, fast-flowing river was the setting for some of Joseph Conrad's earliest novels.

To the east of Bali lies a lengthy chain of islands known by Indonesians as Nusa Tenggara—the "Southeastern Islands." Also known by their geographic name, the "Lesser Sundas," this is one of the least known but most intriguing areas of Indonesia. The chain begins with the islands of Lombok and Sumbawa. These islands are dominated by the Sasak people who are strong Muslim folk with a love of horses. All of these islands lie to the east of the Wallace Line; further to the east the islands of Flores, Sumba and Timor have a characteristically arid landscape influenced by hot and dry winds blasting up from Australia. They are inhabited by a kaleidoscopic variety of tribes, each with their own tongues.

The coastline of Indonesia's eastern islands is wild and breathtaking. The harsh sunlight bounces off dazzling white coral and a seawater so clear that even at depths of 50 meters (160 feet) or more the seabed can easily be seen. Nature's stunning gift to these islands is a purity of light and color. The further east the traveler goes, the more dry and barren the landscape becomes. Approaching the Wallace line the scenery assumes Mediterranean hues and tones. Komodo and Rinca Islands are typical in this regard. The climate is dry, hot, and relatively barren compared to the lush and wooded islands to the east and west of them in the Nusa Tenggara island chain.

Opposite: Komodo Island's magnificent pink beach is a tropical jewel.
Top right: On the island of Lombok the horse remains a valued means of transport.
Bottom right: Beach life looks relaxed for these young boys in Lombok, but they are skilled fishermen at an early age. Their livelihood depends on it.

Komodo Island is the famous home of the world's largest living lizards and is a popular destination for adventurous tourists. The island's famous pink beach is a fabulous spot to dive among living coral reefs. All of Indonesia's far-flung islands offer the visitor splendid views of nature in its purest form. There's also a sense that time has stood still and much of the way life is led here today is little different from the way it was half a century ago.

Indonesia's outer islands are famous for their great lakes and rivers as well. Sumatra and Borneo still hold vast tracts of rain forest that are drained by great rivers. The island of Borneo is perhaps one of the last great natural reserves left in the tropics and is one of the world's green lungs, helping to pump oxygen back into the atmosphere. But this important ecological role is increasingly threatened by illegal logging, which destroys the primary forest, and the spread of palm oil plantations. The disappearing primary rain forest threatens the existence of almost 500 unique bird and animal species which rely on the Borneo forest for their habitat.

Although it's hard to imagine the vast expanse of forest in Indonesia being eradicated, the warnings are growing more urgent and the government is now trying harder to crackdown on illegal logging operations, which these days mostly send valuable hardwood to be turned into plywood for the booming construction industry in China.

Yet beyond the island of Java, strict controls are hard to implement, especially in the country's new era of democracy. A new local autonomy law gives the regions more of a say over their resources and how they are used. After decades of being exploited by the center, many local governments are eager to make up for lost time and rake in revenues from their abundant natural resources—but this means that logging is taking place at a more rampant rate. Another major challenge for Indonesia's most remote regions is their difficult access.

Populations become less concentrated the further east you travel. In parts of West Papua, the new name for Irian Jaya (the western half of the huge island of New Guinea), the population density plunges to around two people per square kilometer. Small planes are often the only way to reach very remote villages in Papua or Kalimantan. Some of these aircraft are operated on a private basis by Christian missionaries who have traditionally been vital links to the outside world.

Air travel is highly developed in Indonesia, with several private airlines now operating with fares that are cheaper than the inter-island ferry service. Turn up at the airport in Jakarta before seven in the morning and you will be able to catch a flight to almost any of Indonesia's far-flung islands. Often the planes are small, and the airstrips rudimentary—although the service is always cheerful.

Otherwise, all people can rely on is the trusty pick-up truck on a dirt track. Riverboats and canoes are used along the country's great rivers. But highways are scarce.

Left: Borneo's fast-flowing rivers make for excellent rafting adventures.
Top right: The same is true of the Alas River in North Sumatra.
Bottom right: Passenger ferries ply the huge island on Lake Toba in North Sumatra.

At the far end of eastern Indonesia is the large island of Papua, also known as New Guinea. West Papua became the twenty-sixth province of Indonesia in 1969 after an "Act of Free Choice", sponsored by the UN, saw the transfer of official administration from The Netherlands. The indigenous people of West Papua are related ethnically and culturally to the Melanesian peoples of the Pacific.

Indonesia's half of this vast island is a wonder world of untamed nature and primitive culture. In the central mountainous region of the province, which takes an hour to cross in a small jet, lies a grand valley some 70 kilometers (43 miles) long and in parts only 16 kilometers (10 miles) wide. The Baliem Valley is inhabited by a throwback to the Stone Age, the Dani tribe. Until a generation ago the Dani people had little to do with the outside world, until the arrival of white missionaries in the 1950s. Even today, the Dani rely on stone axes and on an agricultural lifestyle that revolves around raising pigs and growing root crops.

Much of eastern Indonesia was exposed to the earliest Christian missions to Asia. St Francis Xavier, who also helped bring Christianity to China, was among the first to convert natives in the Maluku Islands in the 16th century. In 1546, Xavier left Malacca on the Malay Peninsula and went

Top left: This Dani tribesman is posing in the Baliem valley with a mummified ancestor and sports one of the only items of clothing that the Dani wear—a penis sheath, or *koteka*.
Bottom left: Short haul aircraft are the only means of penetrating West Papua's remote highlands.
Right: This suspension bridge in the Baliem Valley makes for a precarious means of traversing this wild and remote country.

The magnificent horizon as seen from the island of Ambon in Maluku, which lies at the center of the famed Spice Islands.

A Christian church peeks through the undergrowth in Mamasa, Western Toraja on the huge island of Sulawesi.

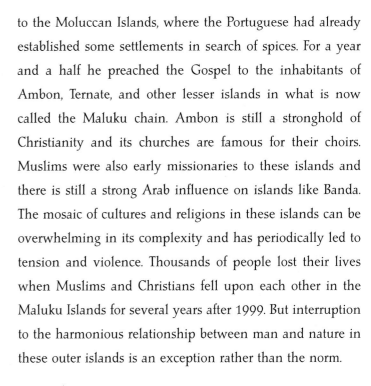

to the Moluccan Islands, where the Portuguese had already established some settlements in search of spices. For a year and a half he preached the Gospel to the inhabitants of Ambon, Ternate, and other lesser islands in what is now called the Maluku chain. Ambon is still a stronghold of Christianity and its churches are famous for their choirs. Muslims were also early missionaries to these islands and there is still a strong Arab influence on islands like Banda. The mosaic of cultures and religions in these islands can be overwhelming in its complexity and has periodically led to tension and violence. Thousands of people lost their lives when Muslims and Christians fell upon each other in the Maluku Islands for several years after 1999. But interruption to the harmonious relationship between man and nature in these outer islands is an exception rather than the norm.

Left: A luminous sunset on a North Sulawesi beach with the Manado Tua volcano looming in the background.

"Do I like life in the tropics? Yes, indeed, I am enchanted with all I see. I enjoy many indescribable sensations of delight..."

— Anna Forbes (1886)

Visiting
Indonesia

If there was a way of spending a lifetime traveling, then a good part of growing up might usefully be spent exploring Indonesia as a visitor. For certainly the experience equips you with a lifetime's worth of stimulation and experience. First there are the people, countless numbers of people with their smiles and always-engaging manner. Then there are the places, a myriad different places, each as fascinating and different from the other. Finally there is the art and culture, embodying a rich, deep sense of beauty and purpose. But no lifetime can be spent without time spent relaxing, and Indonesia is an easy place to lose days, weeks, months, even years with little purpose other than rest and relaxation. Perched on the edge of a landscaped pool overlooking verdant rice terraces sculpted out of a narrow gorge in Ubud, Bali, or exploring the beautiful reefs around Manado in North Sulawesi province, for instance, one feels enveloped by a certain timelessness and there is almost no compulsion to ever leave.

Arguably, Indonesia's greatest natural asset is the sea lying between its thousands of islands. No visitor can escape the sea for long. It envelops everything. Take an Indonesian to a land-locked country and he feels disoriented and uncomfortable. The sea provides sustenance and a sense of insulation, as well as a means of connection with the outside world. There is a continental quality about Indonesia that is hard to grasp given its geography. For the tourist, Indonesia's natural environment is a huge draw. Some of the best diving locations in the world can be found, for example, off the coasts of North Sulawesi or Bali, or in more remote locations off the coast of West Papua. Here the coral reefs teem with marine life hard to see elsewhere. Bali of course is famous for its surf and the social set that congregates along the famous Kuta Beach at sunset.

Yet with so many islands to choose from, there is no shortage of secluded beach life. Indonesia practically gave birth to the idea of the intimate hideaway beach resort with private bungalows set within lush tropical gardens. At night subdued lighting and the gentle tinkle of the gamelan enhances the sense of intimacy.

By day the ocean invites you to take long exploratory dives amongst some of the most varied and colorful sea life found

Page 82: A tourist travels around Lombok on a rented motorcycle—an inexpensive and convenient way to explore the island.
Page 83: Balinese-syle wedding ceremonies held in a lavish tropical setting are popular with Asian and European tourists.
Left: Tourists from a nearby cruise ship enjoy the crystal clear waters and remarkable coral of Komodo island's famed pink beach.
Right: The coast of North Sulawesi near Manado offers one of the best dive sites in the world.

anywhere in the world. By dusk the beach beckons against a contemplative backdrop of spectacular sunsets.

Contemplation is an important part of any visit to Indonesia. This is no place to rush or hustle. The very force of nature slows down the body clock, relaxes the limbs and focuses the mind on deeper matters beyond the mundane rhythms of our existence. It is here that artists and writers flock to seek inspiration. Bali in particular has attracted many artists among them modern European masters like Rudolph Bonnet, Walter Spies, Miguel Covarubbias, Theo Meier and many others. They came in the 1930s when Bali was just being discovered by the outside world and many of their paintings remain on the island displayed in museums.

The art of Indonesia, although influenced by its folk traditions, has assimilated influences from China and Europe to help produce a profusion of styles and schools. Figurative art is popular and many of the artists from Bali and Yogyakarta command high prices at regional auctions.

There is serenity but also a profusion of stimuli, from the intricate plant life of the lush landscape to the azure splendor of its oceans or angular volcanic landscapes.

Indonesia is home to a plethora of ancient forms of healing and natural medication. For more than a thousand years,

Opposite: Thatched-roof holiday bungalows constructed in the shape of traditional Balinese rice barns are a good way to enjoy the bucolic Ubud environment in Bali.
Top right: For splendid scenery and isolation, the Bagus Jati resort located high in the mountains on the road to Kintamani above Ubud is hard to beat.
Bottom right: The landscaping in Bali gardens is enhanced by the skills of its stone carvers and artisans.

Indonesians have used the chemical properties of natural herbs and plants to help cure and prevent common ailments. Unlike modern medicine which attacks infections and viruses, the natural properties of Indonesian herbal preparations, known as *jamu*, encourages the body to produce its own reaction to disease, acting as a catalyst. These herbal powders, usually mixed with water, are not only pedaled as cures for basic ailments like flu, gastric complaints and the like, but are also considered essential beauty aids. Mothers of newborn children take *jamu* to quickly restore the youthful shape of their bodies, while certain types of *jamu* are famous for their ability to make women seem or look more alluring. For men, there is a whole range of male potency enhancers as well.

Traditional Indonesian purveyors of *jamu* walk the streets clad in traditional sarong and kebaya with a basket full of remedies in brightly-colored bottles that are dispensed by the glass. Today, the visitor can enjoy the soothing properties of *jamu* at modern spas and health centers.

Indonesia's natural environment has a calming, restorative effect and the visitor can choose from a growing number of discreet hideaway hotels where the emphasis is on solitude and contemplation. The world is full of chaos and color, and Indonesia has its fair share of riotous, exotic scenery. But for the world-weary there is probably no place on earth where

Top left: Ancient massage therapy relies on a blend of soothing essential oils and relaxing surroundings to enhance the soft touch of the masseuse.
Bottom left: The heat of the day is best fended off with a plunge into a landscaped pool filled with flowers.

Above: Meditation is the perfect antidote for relieving stress and soaking up the serenity of the surroundings.
Right: Indonesia has perfected the art of creating the perfect blend of nature and art in the shape of the hideaway resort hotel.

Above left: The famous hanging graves in Torajaland are a draw for visitors to South Sulawesi.
Above right: Adventure can take the form of an elephant ride through the forests of Bali.
Opposite: Indonesia's fabulous resorts are the perfect setting for every social occasion.

Indonesia boasts some of the world's most sophisticated tropical resorts. From left to right are the Bali Bale, the Bagus Jati and the Four Seasons Resort Sayan, all located in Bali.

stress can be so effectively dissipated. The Balinese or Javanese ancient art of *pijit* (massage) takes the body on a journey back thousands of years to rediscover the aura for the well-being of body and mind. The ancients believed that certain flowers, such as frangipani, magnolia and rose helped relax the soul. They burned incense as an aromatherapy to stimulate the soul and relax the mind. As the muscles begin to relax with the influence of this aromatherapy, the masseuse begins to work the flesh with a selection of soothing herbs and oils. This kind of treatment overcomes the senses and deeply penetrates the soul. When magical fingers start to softly touch the body, everything becomes rhythmic, calm, and fresh with the perfect combination of romantic ambiance and hands of a dancer.

Right: Like so many other things, the resorts of Bali were pioneers in developing a new standard in stylish spa retreats where the stresses of the workaday world quickly melt away.

Left: Indonesia is a riot of arts and crafts and even the simplest of fashion accessories are tempting, like these colorful sandals in Surabaya's Arab quarter.

Clockwise from top left: The painted wayang puppet makes for an eye-catching memento; The shadow puppet is cut from soft leather and is the pinnacle of artisanship in Central Java; A carved Barong mask from Bali; The renowned designer Obin of Bin House creates batik designs on delicate hand-woven silk that offer style at a premium price.

SELECTED FURTHER READING

Bali: Sekala & Niskala Volumes I & II, Fred B. Eiseman, Jr, (Singapore, Periplus Editions, 1990)

Balinese Dance, Drama and Music, I Wayan Dibia and Rucina Ballinger, (Singapore, Periplus Editions, 2004)

Borobudur: Golden Tales of the Buddhas, John Miksic, (Singapore, Periplus Editions, 1990)

Indonesia: Between Myth and Reality, Lee Khoon Choy, (Singapore, Federal Publications, 1977)

Indonesia: Land Under the Rainbow, Mochtar Lubis, (Singapore, Oxford, 1990)

Island of Bali, Miguel Covarrubias, (Singapore, Periplus Editions, 2004)

Jakarta Inside Out, Daniel Ziv, (Jakarta, Equinox Publishing, 2002)

Java Facts and Fancies, August De Wit, (Singapore, Oxford, 1912)

Javanese Culture, Koentjaraningrat, (Singapore, Institute of Southeast Asian Studies, 1985)

Kretek: The Culture and Heritage of Indonesia's Clove Cigarettes, Mark Hanusz, (Jakarta, Equinox Publishing, 2000)

The Malay Archipelago, Alfred Russel Wallace, (Singapore, Periplus Editions 2000)

Nathaniel's Nutmeg: How One Man's Courage Changed The Course of History, Giles Milton, (London, Sceptre Books, 1999)

The Spice Garden: A Novel, Michael Vatikiotis, (Jakarta: Equinox Publishing, 2004)

Tales From Djakarta, Pramoedya Ananta Toer, (Jakarta, Equinox Publishing, 2001)

Unbeaten Tracks in Islands of the Far East: Experiences of a Naturalist's Wife, Anna Forbes, (Singapore, Oxford, 1988)

Welcome to Indonesian, Stuart Robson, (Singapore, Periplus Editions, 2004)